CW00860235

CAPTURED

Bo Rodriguez

Proudly published by blurb

Captured

Bo Rodriguez

 San Francisco, CA

An imprint of Blurb, Inc.

580 California St # 300, San Francisco, CA 94104

Copyright © 2017 Bo Rodriguez Company

580 California St # 300, San Francisco, CA 94104

For information about special discounts or bulk purchases,

please contact The Bo Rodriguez Company

borodriguezcompany@gmail.com

Interior design by Bo Rodriguez

Manufactured in the United States of America

10 9 8 7 6 5 4 3 2

Library of Congress Cataloging- in- Publication data is

available

This signed copy of

CAPTURED

Bo Rodriguez

Bo Rodriguez

Is a part of a limited special edition bond by the author.

Contents

Contents

Contents

Dedications

Dedications

This book is dedicated to the most loving, energetic and hardworking families I know. The Browning and the Pineda Families. These people are the reason I am writing this book because of the education, careers, and families that they have carved for themselves. I find this very impactful and a valuable lesson to me, that it's important to work hard and you will achieve amazing things. Thank you, Tom, Monica, Christen, Danny, Dalia, and Celeste for always being there for me, and inspiring me. I Love you all so much.

-Bo Rodriguez

Intro

Intro

Okay, let me start off by saying that everything in this book is not to embarrass anyone or anything, except for myself. Well, I got that out of the way so let me introduce myself. Hello, random person that I may know, I am Bo Rodriguez a random teenager in Houston, Texas that is conceited, annoying, obnoxious, very blunt, and likes gum. Wow, great introduction.

Now many of you are probably wondering why a teenager would write a book? What the hell could he possibly be writing about, and you know what I would tell you? "Because I freaking wanted to you asshole." I do not think you are an asshole though. Anyways I have wanted to write a book since the fall of two thousand fifteen. However, the main reason I wanted to write a book is because I feel that I'm not very personal and open about my past and what I go through that is amazing and devastating. Being a very closed-minded person,

I hardly talk about big topics or personal and spiritual beliefs and don't worry it's not going to be one of those books!

In my book, you will find a mixture of funny, sad and awkward stories. I hope that you enjoy this book as much as I do. So, before you start reading it I just want to thank you, thank you for supporting me and believing in me on this journey I love you so much, and I am so grateful for you. Okay, the book starts now! GO!

Hi! It me!

Hi! It Me!

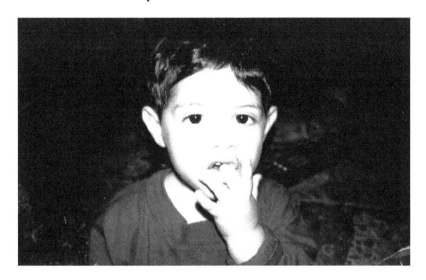

So, you haven't thrown this in the can yet? I guess that's a good thing! So far in this book, you've only read about the dedications and the intro. But you still don't know everything about me, and I know the reason you bought this book was to get to know me a little more. Or this may be your first time getting to know me! So, hey everyone I know, and Hi random stranger! I am Bo Rodriguez. I am not like your average teenager, most teens today play sports, hang out with friends 24/7 or are so invested in an activity that they dedicate all their time and energy into it. Well, I am not the first two, but I am the third one. I am so invested in the book you're holding right now, and hopefully more books to come! I enjoy doing the following hobbies; I like to do crafts, I like to write, I like to over think and I love to sleep. Yes, you heard me right. I like to sleep. You know that thing that doctors recommend you get about eight hours of each night. Yes, that is a hobby, if it's something you like and you do it in your free time, then it's a hobby. Anyways, I am fifteen years old at the time of writing this, and I go to Lamar High School in Houston, Texas. I have no comment on the school I am just telling you where I go.

So as a little tot I was petty as fuck. I needed everything to pretty much be sanitized, and I could never be in a dirty diaper as a baby for longer than thirty seconds. Why didn't my parents get rid of me? I don't know. I was also very into Cars and Thomas the train. My collection of those toys could probably wrap around the world two times. I remember every birthday and Christmas all I wanted were Cars and trains.

I don't know why but I loved that stuff, and honestly, I still like Cars.

As far as my wardrobe I was very stylish. I loved to wear striped shorts with a striped shirt. I would also wear sponge bob themed Hats, shirts, shorts, socks, underwear, and flip-flops. I was a fashion icon, And just very cringe-worthy. Obviously, by now I have changed my wardrobe, now I only have the same shirt from Urban Outfitters but in assorted colors, and I like to wear tight black sweatpants from Forever 21 and white Vans. That's my go-to look.

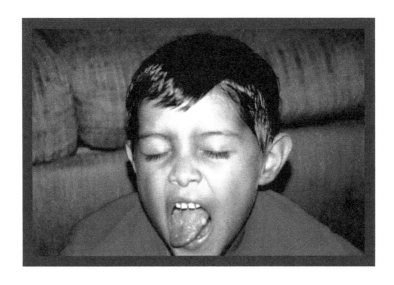

Who Is Bo?

Who Is Bo?

Well, I'm Bo, but that's obviously not my name. My names are,

-Rolando

-Ronald

-Rollie

-Bo

But I prefer Bo over any of the other names. Just because I want to be a white boy with blonde hair and blue eyes duh. No, I'm just kidding. Kind of. But a lot of people get confused when they hear my name said, This is because everyone calls me a different name. If you were to put five people in a room, they will probably each say a different name. So, I went to Google Because the internet is always right. And I came along a very sketchy website that had subjective definitions of everyday words. And my name was in there! The next page has the meanings of my name.

TOP DEFINITION

Bo

B.O, body odour. A nice smelling smell that you get if you don't shower regulary and sweat a lot.
Pronounced as BEE-OH

Woah, who smells of B.O?

by j00l.i.e April 26, 2003

Bo

A Bo is strong, handsome, noble, masculine, with a burning disire to succeed. Flexible, but does not break. Extremely capable, knowledgeable, positive, certian, never boastful. An unbreakable will. Bo knows what it takes to win and will push it to the very edge, if thats not enough, Bo will push it over the edge. Bo believes there is no such thing as a second place winner. Easy does it,,,my ass.

Bo

coolest mother fucker ever

damn look at bo

by bo bona June 11, 2003

Personally my favorite is Definition number 3.

Family

Family

So, as you know, I was born and raised in Houston Texas to Parents Janie Rodriguez and Rolando Rodriguez. I have three amazing sisters that I would do anything for; Conchita, Connie, and Sofia Rodriguez. My parents and siblings are the most important thing to me. Yes, I wrote a book, yes, I go to school and do my very best. But I will always care about my family more than anything.

Growing up with sisters as much as I love them can be hard. There was a lot of pink, glitter, and Barbie's. All our bedrooms were in the same hallway, all my sister's bedrooms were either pink and purple. And then there's my bedroom. The only Blue, green, red, cars themed bedroom. You would think that I was adopted. But even though my sisters were obviously not into the same things that I was. We finally got our hands on a piece of technology. We got a play station. And man did we use that thing. One direction who? We were our own band with games called rock band and guitar hero. And obviously I

had a Disney cars game on their cause I was addicted to
cars, kind of Like a white boy high school student is to his
JUUL. I'm kidding, kind of. But playing on the play
station obviously got dated, so I believe it was Christmas
of 2008 that my Mom and dad got a Wii. And oh my god
that was probably the best gaming device that they ever
invested in. Except for the game that was about fitness
and yoga I hated that game.

    The year that I think me and my sisters were most
close was 2009. In 2009 my parents were going through a
divorce. So, our stay at home mom, was not a stay at
home mom anymore cause she had to work to support
herself and the four of us. That summer we were a roller
coaster of emotions whether we were Happy cause we
weren't thinking of the divorce, or we were sad cause of
the divorce. Or we were just pissed off because we didn't
understand. In the Fall of 2009, my sisters and I found
out that our dad had won custody of us. And I remember
being devastated. I did not want to live with my dad. And
he knows that. I have nothing against him I just think
that children need their mothers more than their fathers,

That's just my opinion, and I have thought that since 2009. So, my sisters and I continued to live with my father in La Porte Texas. Proceeded to go to La Porte Independent school district. And I disliked everything from there on out. I did not want to live in La Porte. I was so stubborn with my dad that sometimes I would stay with my mom a little longer because I didn't want to go back to my dad's. The only reason I had to go back was for school. But my sisters Sofia, Connie and I continued to live they're throughout the summer of 2014. I remember the exact day and what happened. My dad and I were talking, and he was just so rude, as was I. That I had enough of living there, I told him I was going to move in with my mom.

31

Awkward

Bo Rodriguez

Awkward

As a child, I did a lot of weird stuff. I never really cared what I was doing. I never realized that what I was doing was incredibly cringe-worthy. But I guess I was comfortable and never really cared. I remember precisely what I was thinking in this photo,

"Why is the water so green, why is that kid looking at me, I wonder what we're having for dinner tonight, And I think I have to use the restroom, so I'm just going to make this weird, uncomfortable face." Being awkward is okay. But personally, I hate being awkward it's one of my biggest fears. Well, that and something crawling in my ear and laying eggs and then I die.

Preschool Drama

Preschool Drama

Oh, this is a good one. Everyone as a child loves preschool! It's fun because you color, play with other kids and nap. That's a four-year-old dream. Well not for me! I HATED preschool. When I was four, I was the most prominent germaphobe. I did not like to be dirty, Smell dirty. Or wear an outfit for too long. I was every parent's nightmare. I hated preschool cause four-year-olds are disgusting! They pick their noses, eat it and are always touching themselves you would think they were a teenager! You know what I mean, there just gross. I'm surprised I didn't go to school with a medical mask, medical gloves, or a germ suit.

Well one of the many activities that we had (Remember that word had) to do was finger paint. I was not for this. I loved to paint but with a brush. The way it is supposed to be done. Well, this Bitch of a teacher forced me to finger paint, and of course, I'm having a meltdown. I remember I kept asking her, "Can I just paint with a brush

Mrs. Bitch?" And she gave me so much attitude because I asked that. So, I refused to paint and told her to fuck off. And to not touch me! Oh, my lord, she was horrible! So, I walked my four-year-old self right down to the front office of this small atrocious preschool. I told the receptionist what happened and shed a tear. She felt terrible and called either my mom or dad I can't remember because of that teacher. So, once she was off the phone, I went and sat on a bench in the front office and witnessed this mother and a young boy trying to enroll with another receptionist. When she sat down I said;

> Me: I would not fill out that paperwork...
>
> Woman: Why sweetie?
>
> Me: A teacher forced me to finger paint when I asked her if I could just paint with the brush that I had. And she made me cry.
>
> Woman: Got up and left.

Once my dad arrived at the school I was done crying. He proceeded to ask what happened, even though he knew.

- Captured -

He got pissed. Not at me, but at this horrible preschool. So, on that early morning in 2005 I had dropped out of school. Well not really, me and my dad joke that I just graduated early. And of course, this wouldn't be a story if I didn't @ the school. So, @ Asbury Methodist Day School in Pasadena, Texas what's good?

The time I almost died

The time I almost died

Who hasn't almost died? Maybe in a car crash, scared to death, or even just doing something so normal like choking on food. That one happens to me way too often. While yes all of these have happened to me. That's not what this story is about. This story is about the time I hit my head on my sister's head, and we almost died.

Oh goodness, where do I begin... Around kindergarten, I was a very imaginative child. I liked toy cars and trains and pretending I was a car. (Keep that in mind.) With me being very imaginative I always had a vision of a road or a railroad track in my home. And I always, would stop at the lights, stop signs, and when people would want to cross the street. You would think that I was on crack cocaine. But I was not. One night I was with my three sisters and my mother. My father was on his way, back from work. We had an average day went to school, and my mother was preparing our dinner. And mind you, while she was doing that I was in Bo's world pretending I was a car. So as a car, I had technical problems, and basically, I had to Pee which I would compare to "my car leaking gas". So, I zoomed to my mom and dad's bathroom to pee because I felt like being "premium" (gas joke). So, While I was zooming, I noticed my sister Connie running at full speed out of the bedroom. And I didn't react fast enough, and I was having brake problems. And that resulted in both of us having a front head collision.

All I remember was being on the floor, and something was dripping down my face. And that was blood. I had cut my head open, and blood was pouring out. I remember hearing my older sister Conchita, and just sitting on the couch with a towel over my head. My mom was on the phone with my dad and was very calm but naturally super concerned. A few minutes passed I think, and my dad was home. My mom knew I needed stitches, and so did my dad. So, we immediately got into the car and headed to the emergency room. My sister Connie was in the car as well; she didn't cut her head open she was just in pain from us running into each other.

When we arrived at the emergency room, there were like a million people in there. So, we had to wait. And from here I can't remember the story very well. I know I got put into a tortilla (they wrapped me in like a blanket) and they gave me stitches. Oh, and the best part, was that I got excused from my gym class for like two months. My year was made!

The time I peed on myself

In kindergarten, I was innocent, brown, and a clean freak. I hated germs or anything that was dirty on my body. And honestly, nothing has changed. Like my past chapter about the teacher who made me finger paint is an excellent example of why I hate getting dirty and why that woman is a C U Next Tuesday. However, I also never liked to use the restroom at school cause, Ew. Ew. I still to this day have not used a school restroom unless it is a complete emergency like I have to pee, but never to poo. So, by now you probably know where this story is going.

One day at recess this new play set had been installed, it had three red slides with a yellow fire pole that was twisty. It looked exactly like a taco bell cinnamon twist. Ugh, those were my favorite. Anyway, I decided that I wanted to swing down that pole like the striper I am and make this a performance. So, I sat with my legs wrapped around the pole and started to spin around. About halfway down I felt something warm going down my legs, and into my shoes. I bet you guessed it, I was full on peeing on myself. So, at this point, my urine is all over me and all over that pole. It was like if magic mike had pissed everywhere. Once I finally made my way around the pole, I immediately thought, "what am I going to do?" because I couldn't go back to class smelling like urine.

So, I walked to my teacher who is the sweetest woman in the entire world, and I told her, "Mrs. Jobe I accidentally peed on myself and the play set." She didn't make a scene she directed me to the side entrance of the school, and asked a lovely friend of mine at the time to walk me down to the school nurse. So, we walked to the nurse, and I remember having to wear these ugly blue jeans and this collared shirt with anchors on it. Honestly, 10/10 would not recommend that shirt. But since I was an enormous germaphobe when I was little I was freaking out about all the kids that have probably worn that shirt. It was

-Bo Rodríguez-

a Horrible day, horrible smell, and horrible outfit.

Birthdays

Birthdays

Oh, birthdays. Or I like to call them one year closer to death! I am not a very huge fan of my birthday. There are many reasons for this. I don't like to have a day where I am the center of attention because I'm socially awkward. But also, my birthday is on the fourth of July, so everyone wants to be patriotic and watch fireworks. And every year I tell my family I just want to relax at home and have a nice dinner with them, but at last minute I always decide to have close family and close family friends over which I love. For many years

I would celebrate my birthday in California with the close family members that I have there. I loved having my birthday in California. The weather is beautiful, and I loved just going on planes. Except for the night before I always freak out that the plane will crash and I'll die. Why am I thinking that as a six-year-old? I am not sure. Anyways I use to celebrate my birthday at My grandparent's homes, whether it was my fathers mom and dad, or my mothers mom and dad. I have never had a birthday at my house growing up as a little tot.

The reason is that I didn't have that many friends in elementary school, I bounced around in diverse groups throughout elementary. Having said this, I never invited nor got invited to birthday parties. So, I would always have my birthday at their homes because all my cousins and aunts and uncles would go. I loved having my birthdays there, but I still wanted to have my birthday with friends. Now I don't really care, It's just a birthday. But to anyone that has been to any of my little birthday "parties" just know that I appreciate and love you!

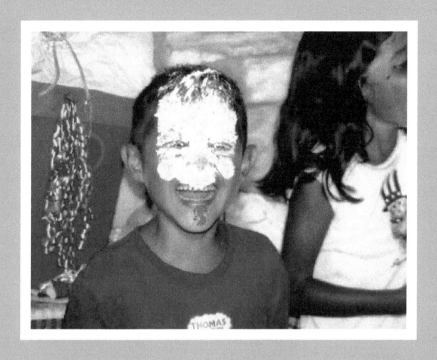

The time I drowned

The time I drowned

I drowned. I remember the day like it was yesterday. It was my cousin, (for the sake of privacy we're going to call this cousin Eric Rodriguez) and me. Well, Eric knew how to swim and would in a way show off. And I did not know how to swim, ride a bike let alone know anything about physical activity. So I had no idea that you had to know how to "swim" I thought you were able to touch the floor throughout the entire pool. Well, my dumbass jumped directly into the pool, and my ass sank to the bottom. I remember drinking all of that nasty community pool urine, not water, Urine. Yes, I was chugging that disgusting urine water, thinking this is how I am going to die, and then I legit blacked out.

About ten minutes later I felt something burning my back. It was the concrete and someone blowing air into my mouth. It was a male lifeguard that was giving me mouth to mouth. "Never knew my first kiss was going to be with a boy but okay"- 5-year-old Bo. All I remember after getting maked out with was sitting on a white pool chair and eating grapes

I'm such a good storyteller.

The time I learned

how to swim

The time I learned how to swim

What a historic day. It should be a holiday. The day I
learned how to swim. Also the same summer I learned how to
ride a bike. So I was in a surrounding city in San Diego
visiting one of my favorite aunts. My Aunt Monica, Uncle
Tom, and cousin Chrissy. My favorite people on this planet
and I hardly see them. Well anyways I was at their old house,
and they had one of the most amazing pools I have ever seen.
It had dark beautiful tile and it was always nice and cold.
Well one day while we were visiting them my family had the
idea of going swimming, but I didn't know how to swim. So
my dad was like your going to learn today. So he started off
with me jumping into the pool and him catching me. I was
terrified I'm pretty sure I was peeing mid-jump. Sorry Dad.
He then held my hands and told me to kick so that I could
move. This was the most exercise I had ever done.

- Captured -

Then he let go. And I wasn't drowning. I was so surprised that I almost drowned. But I swam across the entire pool by myself! Without floaties! I felt like I had won the Olympics. Michael Phelps who? No, I'm kidding, but I was proud of myself, and so was my dad. And that is one of my favorite moments that I've ever had with him. Ouch my heart. ;(

The time I played a sport

The Time I played a sport

Yes, what you read is true. I have played a sport. And it was baseball, and it was an interesting time in my life. I've never been a big sports person I still don't know how football, soccer or any other sport for that matter work. The only sport that I can comprehend is Baseball. But that's cause I "played it"

I remember the day like it was yesterday. Tryouts. I was confident I wouldn't make any team, but apparently when your eight everyone who tries out gets in. So obviously at tryouts, I almost shit myself cause I was so nervous. But at the same time, I didn't care, cause I didn't even want to play. Well, I made the team. I played on the Pirates, in La Porte Texas at a baseball field near my house And I was not sure how I felt. I didn't want to play, but my parents had already paid, so I kind of had to play.

The time I played a sport   Bo Rodriguez

So once we got to know everyone on the team, we got assigned our positions. I was assigned an outfielder which was great! Cause I didn't have to pay attention to the game. I could just daydream, and no one would know. Unless an eight-year-old hit the ball and that shit flew across the field. And also I was like horrible at batting, so I never batted, unless there was no one else to do so. But like I said earlier I didn't care to play. I didn't even want to be there.

It was one of our last games And we were losing by one point, and it was the last inning. So stupidly they assigned me to bat. I was losing my shit. Even though I didn't care about playing I didn't want to one embarrass myself, and have me be the reason I loss the game. So I was preparing to bat when my teammate hit the ball and ran to first base. So I was freaking out if I get striked out that's it. Cause we already had two outs. So I went to home plate and missed the first throw, then the next. So I stepped back and took a breath. When the pitcher threw the ball, I hit that ball a little behind second base. It was

The time I played a sport   Bo Rodriguez

Honestly like Chicken Little when he hasn't realized he hit the ball, and doesn't know which way to run. I took off I ran all the way to first base, but someone threw the ball to first base a second before I got there. So yeah I made the team lose but like I got a baseball that night signed by all the coaches.

So even though I'm not a fan of sports, I'm glad that the pirates was the first team, and last team I was ever on.

Almost getting kidnapped

Almost getting Kidnapped

Before I start this chapter I just want to say that I don't find this topic funny, or amusing nor was my experience entertaining, the following story was a real event that I hope will not offend anyone. Now that I got that out of the way lets start this crazy story. So when I was a tiny tot, I played baseball. I know shocker. But I did, when I was in second grade, I played on the pirates as an outfielder or something like that I'm not entirely sure. Well, I hated it so much I was more a boy scout boy which I enjoyed very much. Well, continuing my story I was getting ready for some stupid game that I didn't want to do or be a part of, but my parents had already paid for it, so I had to play.

So I went to put my equipment in the back of my dads very green Honda Accord that was older than I was. While I was putting my stuff in the trunk of the accord I was doing what any eight year old would do, just playing in the front yard waiting for my dad to say let's go. While I was playing by myself in the front yard, I noticed this creepy old Ford truck that was a light blue color slowly approaching me. Me being a child who knew what stranger danger meant, I didn't even listen to that statement while this was happening. So he stopped right in front of my house where I was, and I just stood there confused thinking, what the hell does this creepy old man want? So he sat in his car and just started a conversation. He asked so many questions that at the time I didn't find alarming. He asked what team I was on, Where and when was the game, And how old I was. So me being the idiot I am told him all the information.

He wished me the best of luck and then started to drive off. My mom must have seen me talking to him, and she came out and started yelling at me. She told me that I obviously should have known better and so on. So random man that could have kidnapped me, I hope you're doing well, and I hope you made it back to Oklahoma well. Cause I still have your license plate memorized.

The time I was in Cub Scouts

The time I was in Cub Scouts

Oh, Cub Scouts. This was my favorite out of school activity that I have ever done. I hated sports, so this was the alternative option. I loved Cub scouts so much, I met so many amazing people, for privacy reasons I don't want to say names but if your reading this you know who you are. But we always did enjoyable activities! I know these might sound lame, but they are some of my favorite memories ever. We would have camping trips in parks. I threw up on a tire swing so... yeah, that was fun! We also would go to retirement homes and oh my god I would get in my feelings. Cause they were all so sweet, friendly and loving. I loved this one woman, and I remember she wasn't there one time and I got really sad. This was the

first time someone I cared about had passed away. She was old, and She was terrific. I don't remember her name, but I remember exactly what she looked like.

    We would also do activities where we had to create a car, boat. And we had races. My dad always invented them, and of course, they were amazing, and we would win. My mom was heavily involved in my cub scouts, she was a troop leader. It was cool for me to have my mom involved in cub scouts, cause she was very supportive of my sisters in swim and softball. But in conclusion, my cub scout years were pretty great. And it is one of my favorite memories that I have.

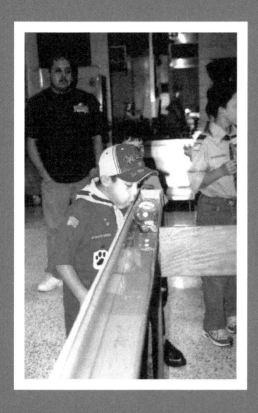

Arya

Arya

So my family has a dog. Her name is Arya, and she is very special. She is not very friendly to other animals unless it is Hank who is an Australian shepherd who walks with his owners, David and Anne. Arya adores them. This chapter will probably be the main selling point for this book because it is about an animal. Who doesn't love animals? Oh, my mother.

Now I bet you're wondering how old Arya is? When did we get her? Well, story-time get a snack I'll wait. Okay, are you ready? Okay great. So it all started when my mother and Jessica (my mother's boyfriends daughter) were visiting a family member. They were going to get into the car when this little nasty brown thing crawled onto Jessica's foot. She instantly fell in love with her and wanted to help her. At the time Arya had mange, fleas, worms, she had little to no hair, she was dehydrated. She was in a life-risking situation. So Jessica the animal lover she is started to ask my mother if she could take Arya home. My mother was conflicted but finally settled on the decision to take her cause if they wouldn't have, what would have happen to her?

So they took Arya and immediately took her to the veterinarian. Arya was in desperate need of medical attention. She needed many tests ran, medications to be put on and a healthy diet and exercise routine. Although she was in the horrible condition, she was still full of energy and just a happy puppy. I recently went to pick up her vet records, and she had over ten visits in a month and was on a few medications, While she was in horrible living conditions.

At the time of writing Arya is a three year old Dog, is still full of energy, and loves her family. And I love her very much.

Moving in with my Mom

Moving in with my Mom

The year I moved in with my mom was the summer of 2014. I remember that I had just had enough of living with my dad that I just left. And I didn't go back or talk to him for a good two months. My dad is a great guy I just cant live with him. The year I moved in with my mom she was leasing a house in Deer Park, Texas. It was a four bedroom two bathroom old house, that had been renovated. And obviously, the renovations were horrible. My mom had a one year lease and then wanted to move back to Houston. She also wanted us to finish the current school year, where we attended school and then transfer us the fall of 2015. Living in that house was very interesting because it was the first house that I lived at with just my mom and the first house that I've lived in with my mom after the divorce. Living with my mom was different because we were all in double digits now, so we had changed since 2009.

- Captured -

My mom had also altered too since she had been introduced to many new things, that her approach to things we grew up with were no longer looked at anymore. But living with my mom has made me more happy and fat. Not a good joke.

Relationships

Nothing lol.

Siblings

Siblings

So you briefly know about my family, but I want to focus on my siblings. Now I don't have any brothers I only have sisters. Which is fine I guess. Earlier this year when I announced that I was writing a book. One of my sisters, Conchita asked if it was an exposé. I informed her that the entire book was not, but this chapter is. So Conchita Welcome to your page.

Oh, Concepcion. A page can not describe how I feel about you. Conchita at the time of writing this just turned 21, so she's an "adult." No, I'm kidding, but I think she was really excited to become twenty-one. She was the first of her friends to be twenty-one... so you know.... Anyway's so as a little tot Conchita swam in her local swim team from third grade to her senior year in high school. She loved to swim, I personally didn't get it. I would just go for the food. But she was very good at her meets!

However, as children, me and Conchita did not really get along. We would bicker and pick heads. It was not a very good sibling relationship. We acted as if we were two bitchy teenage girls in high school. In fact! We did not get along until I was in eighth grade. The year I moved in with my mom was the year we had a better sibling relationship. I think this was due to no longer living in the same home. And we weren't really talking. So I missed her a lot, and I think that it showed in both of us. I remember at the beginning of high school when she was still not living with us, she said "I want a hug," AND I think that's when it really hit me that I needed her around every day Since she is someone that I really care about, and love.

My next sibling is Connie. Connie, Connie, Connie. You are the one that inspired me to cut my own hair. Let me explain. So when Connie and I were little, she took me into Conchita's closet. It was like Connie's ratchet salon. She took scissors and started snipping away, and me gullible just let it happen, and it was free so... I remember my mother being upset with her but I didn't know why. I said "mom why are you upset? I just got a free haircut!"

Connie and I are one year apart but annoy the crap out of each other. And by each other, I mean that I annoy her. She never annoys me. But like I annoy everyone which is a bad hobby. But yeah I love Connie, and I think that she is an amazing sister and person. Also, she is so freaking tall so It like she's a skyscraper, and I'm the dumpster next to her.

Oh, now my favorite. Sofia! I love Sofia so much! She is the girl version of me just a little bitchier. Sofia is someone I can say anything too. Sofia is also the only person that can make me wheeze when I laugh. She is super funny by just doing stupid things. One time we went to garner state park in July just for a small vacation, and she kept saying "Shut up" in a deep man's voice, and I was dying. It's not really funny unless you were there. But anyways she always comes with me when I go see a show or even to the store. Cause we'll just laugh the entire time.

Well, Sofia loves 5SOS, I thought that was like the new Siri update... She loves the television show Supernatural. And loves spicy chips. She swam for a couple of years and did softball as well. Finally, Sofia is a wonderful sister, and I absolutely don't know what I would do without her. Because she is one of the few people that can make my day. I love all my sisters, there all amazing, and I love that they are my sisters. Cause shit I don't know what the hell I would do without them.

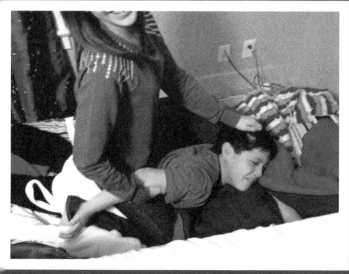

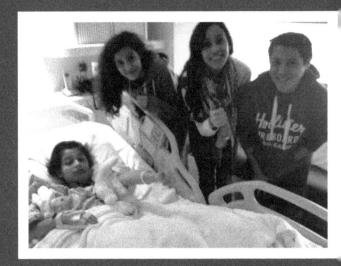

The time I

cheated

Bo Rodriguez

The time I cheated

This is obviously not about a relationship clearly if you read the previous chapter. It's about something way more important. School. You know jail's sister. I'm kidding! But I feel that everyone has cheated in school at least once. That is not even arguable. Cause literally everyone has done it! So don't even be like " I have never cheated on anything in school" Cause I'll know your fucking lying.

Oh, where do I start? So during my sophomore year of high school, I was in Algebra II, And was I confused? Oh hell yeah! (Jenna Marbles voice) Math is my worst subject. In algebra, I sat with my friend Alyssa, and she had attempted to explain what the unit topic was. And I could not for the life of me comprehend it. So about 15 minutes later we were instructed to open our school laptops and begin the test or the "daily grade" So at this point I am freaking out. I can feel my heart racing, and my hands getting clammy. So I started questioning what am I going to do?

The time I cheated

Bo Rodriguez

So I cheated. And of course I missed two questions on purpose, so it didn't look like I knew everything. But that ended up backfiring. My teacher came up to me and asked me to solve a problem that was on that test. I had no idea what to do. I was so scared. I HATE CONFRONTATION! I remember exactly what he said "Rolando, I need you to solve this problem for me. I need to see if you know what you are doing." which meant he figured out that I cheated. I just told him that I couldn't do it, so he gave me a zero. He proceeded to email my mother that I had cheated and said the highest grade I could get was a fifty if I were to retake it. So YOU BET I studied my ass off for the next two days trying to figure that entire unit.

So if you ever decided to cheat which I don't recommend it. Write every little thing you need. Or just Google how to cheat cause I'm not trying to get in trouble.

The time I got detention

The Time I got detention

Oh, this is a goodie. Now for privacy reasons, this story is changed up cause I respect the teacher that was involved, but at the same time she was a bitch. So the teacher's fake name will be Ms. Tree.

I remember the day vividly. It was the Monday students go back to school after spring break. In this class, we had a project. The project intended to create a product or service that could help students, with a specific class. I had the grading rubric, and it said to have the first portion of the project completed, by the Monday following spring break. I believe that the part was creating the name of the product/service, and just having a bit of information about what your planning on doing. Well, I had all of that. But oh no Ms.Tree was not having it, she said I did everything wrong and that I was missing a significant part. But I wasnt cause I had talked to a few friends and asked if it looked okay and they said that it looked great. I did not talk back to Ms. Tree all I asked was, "what I was missing and what she didn't like?" She did not like that question. So she proceeded to give me an academic detention, Where I had to stay after school for like two hours and complete the entire project. So with respect, I said yes ma'am.

When I left her class, I yelled bitch and gave her the finger. Obviously, while I was out of the classroom.

I hate her.

Apple

Apple

Apple has changed everything. In my opinion, they had the best touchscreen phone out in 2007, have amazing computers, and are just so aesthetically pleasing. I love apple I like to have every new product if it's a reasonable price. I always have paid for the products with birthday gift money or as a Christmas gift. I never just ask for it, except when I got my first iPhone, from my mother. This was such a monumental moment. I had wanted one for year's. My older sister's had them for a couple of year's, and I thought I was of age to have a phone.

So that Christmas I asked for an iPhone, and my mom thought that it was a reasonable gift since I didn't have a phone at the time. So she got me a, space gray iPhone 5S with 32 Gigabytes of storage. I loved that phone so much that I managed to shatter it three times! Yes! That's right! And I had to pay to replace them each time. But it was my fault, so I completely understood. But I just love apple! I recently bought the airpods, and a new

Apple watch and and I Completely love them. I love that the products are so easy to use and connect seamlessly. Idk I just really like apple. And yes I'm an apple sheep.

Heres a pic of me getting my first Iphone!

The time I met Colleen Ballinger

The time I met Colleen Ballinger

The time I met Colleen Ballinger! most people know her as Miranda Sings, I know her as amazing. You may be asking yourself, Who the hell is Colleen Ballinger? Colleen Ballinger is a Youtube personality that created her wacky, and delusional alter ego Miranda Sings. Colleen has appeared with the Likes such as Jerry Seinfeld, Jimmy Fallon, Martin Short. She is a rising Youtube personality with millions of online followers. She tours the world with her one-woman show. She has her own Netflix Original series called Haters Back Off which has two seasons. She is an author of a New York Times Bestselling book Selp Helf. And all around a hilarious and successful comedian.

- Bo Rodriguez -

I have been watching Colleen for about four years now, and I am obsessed with her she is super funny and a genius. So in late 2015 when I heard she was going on tour with her former spouse I knew that I had to go and meet her. So I called my dad and told him that all I wanted for Christmas were tickets, and he said as long as my grades were good, and I was good he would get them. So I was able to get them. And I remember having this huge dilemma if the tickets were VIP or just general admission. It did not say either on the ticket. So, of course, I made my mom call the day before to see if they were. She called me, and I almost died because they were VIP. I ONLY HAD ONE DAY TO MENTALLY PREPARE MYSELF!

The day I met Colleen was January 16, 2016, at The University of Houston at there Cullen Performance Hall. I was freaking out. I felt like I was about to shit on myself. And the day was already quite shitty cause it was raining and it was FREEZING. My little sister Sofia went with me, and she was excited, but I don't think she was as excited the way I was. I mean I was the follower that has watched each video at least four times, and know her internet personality up and down. So I was more excited. I still remember exactly what I wore. I wore this blue jacket from Urban Outfitters that I freaking loved (got too big for it, so I donated it) A white shirt from Urban Outfitters, black jeans, and Converse.

So we were in the venue. The meet and greet backdrop was up, and I was freaking out. When Colleen and Kory came out, I was freaking out. I would forget to breathe. Yes, I forget to breathe sometimes. Some other people came out, but they are irrelevant now. Well anyways She did a little Q&A, and then we started taking pictures. I was one of the first ones, and I was shooketh. I was super awkward when I met her it was awful. But I could not stop smiling cause she means so much to me! Colleen is so funny, she is really pretty, and she is very successful. She is one of the few YouTubers that has had two seasons of her own show, tours around the world and has an actual talent. I think that she is amazing. I also met her again at the beginning of 2017 when she did the "Miranda sings live... Your welcome" tour! And I was not awkward we had a full conversation about how I adore her lol! But yea I think that she

is fantastic! If you haven't, you should check out her
YouTube channels!

Selfies

Selfies

Oh, selfies. Such a millennial thing to talk about. Okay, I hate that comment because I see people ages fifty and up taking selfies so don't come at me. Anyways I feel like selfies have changed everything. On social media its the first thing people look at when they judge you, I mean when they go to your profile. So it has to be perfect. It has taken me over four year's to learn how to take a mediocre selfie. Usually, people would say find your best side and good lighting, and for some reason, mine is the left side of my face if it's on the front camera. If I'm taking a selfie with the back camera, the right side of my face is the better side. WHY IS IT SO DIFFICULT. The one thing I hate about taking pictures is that I always look bigger than I think I am. So I still have to remind myself that a camera always adds extra pounds, to make me feel better. And obviously these pictures are horrible, but there's only so much I can do. And if your ugly like me it's tough.

Wow I just wrote a chapter about selfies #WTF

The time Jenna

Marbles found me

funny.

_____

Jenna Marbles   Bo Rodriguez

The time Jenna Marbles found me funny.

YouTube, what an interesting website where people can be who they want. Well, and of course there's weird stuff but I mean there's bizarre shit everywhere. So it was around the end of July in 2015 when Jenna Marbles posted her new "sexual Wednesday" video, but they always come out on Thursdays. No shade just throwing out facts. Well, anyways I was watching her new video that was titled "Helium Booth Tag" FT: Julien Solomita, her boyfriend. The video is hilarious if you haven't watched it, WATCH IT you will piss yourself from how funny that video is, or any of her videos. So there was a specific part where she was making these weird faces, and her voice was super deep, and she was interpreting the Miss America wave, and I was dying of course. However, I looked

Closely and realized she looked like a relative that I know. So being a fourteen year old on social media, I screen-shotted the screen where she looked like one of my family members and tweeted it to her. Apparently she found the tweet funny because she liked and followed me. And she kept liking a couple of my tweets from that week.

Honestly probably one of the most hilarious moments that has ever happened to me. Oh, and when we were driving in California a couple of Days later, I saw her, with her red hair, and her boyfriend with his man bun driving down Sepulveda a major street in Los Angeles. So yeah that happened. Oh, and I will never say what relative it looked like. Cause that would be offensive.

Bo
@BoRodriguez123

@Jenna_Marbles I died this morning watching this and you kinda look like my aunt there

4:33 PM - 30 Jul 2015 from Los Angeles, CA

2 Retweets **6** Likes

♡ ⟲ 2 ♡ 6 ᶁᶥ

Friends

Friends

So i'm going to be really honest. I don't really have that many friends. I have a group of like 20 people that I can tell anything too and trust. But sadly I don't talked to some of them anymore, just cause everyone does different things and go to different schools. I love the friends that have stood by me and sticked with me through everything, From just having family issues, health issues or just friend issues. The people that have sticked by me and have let me just vent to them are, Catherine Saenz, Kacey Reynolds, Diego Rojas, Luke Torres, Katrina Lopez, Ian Hill, Anna Pascali, Surina Belk-Gupta, Mirca Romero, Laura Morales, Dannale Houser, Demi Michelle, Claire Lily, Abbey Thorne, Ronella Augustin, Emely Victorio, Christine Wiggins, Danny Ngyuen, and Tania Gibbs. Are people that I love, and I know that I may not say it. But I hope they know that I do.

In Elementary school I didn't have a best friend. I just

became friends with the people who sat at my table the first week and talked to them. But at the beginning of a new school year I would loose them so I would have to start all over. That always upset me. Cause I wasn't a mean kid I was just a little weird I guess. And no one wanted to stick with me throughout elementary. I never hung out with other kids my age, never got invited to birthday parties, never got invited to sleepovers, and never wanted my own birthday party cause I knew none of my "friends" in elementary school would go. I remember my family always asking me. "Why don't you ever have friends over?" And I would just come up with this joke

"Oh well, I've seen them every day for the past ten months. I need a break, and They can be annoying sometimes."

When in reality I wanted to have friends over. I just didn't have good friends at the time, and I'm just going to put this out there, I care about everyone that has been in my life, and that is the god's honest truth. But Not everyone who has been in my life has cared about me.

I didn't make actual friends that I could tell stuff too and trust until about seventh grade. In Seventh Grade, I met this girl named Kacey Reynolds. At first, I thought she was going to be rude or stuck up. But she will never be compared to that. Kacey is authentic, and I consider her my white sister. I love Kacey so much, there are so many things I have told her that no one else knows. Whether its something about me, someone else or even my book. She is always the first to know. My relationship with Kacey is something I had never had before. We are always laughing and smiling. But, when I moved away from La Porte in 2015 that all changed.

Because Kacey and I no longer went to school with each other. That was one of the hardest things not seeing her every day. Since I have moved to Houston, I have only seen Kacey five times. That is so sad. We occasionally talk on the phone and through social media, but it's not the same. And I know that she is happy, Healthy, and successful in school, but I miss her a lot. And I hope she knows that. I love you, Kacey! <3

Another friend that has been there literally since the day I was born. Is Catherine Saenz. Catherine is someone I've known my entire life, but we got super close in seventh grade. Catherine is also someone I can say anything too! She is a big inspiration with her being confident about her singing, poems, and music. She is fantastic! She is one of the few people that I know that aren't scared to express who they are and be proud of it. She is a kind-hearted, talented, and great friend. I don't know what I would do if I didn't have Catherine Saenz. I love you, Catherine, <3

And to all my other amazing friends that I mentioned. Know that your amazing and that I'm so happy to call all of you my friends. I love all of you so much! <3

Thank you

Wow you finished it! I hope that you liked my first book Captured! I really appreciate that you took the time to read my weird book! I am so grateful for you! Hopefully this is just the start of me writing books! I wish to continue making books! But I cant do it alone! So... If you liked this book share it on Social media with the hashtag

#Borodriguezbook

And share your favorite part of the book!Thanks again!

- Bo Rodriguez

Acknowledgments

Mom

Mom, Thankyou for being so supportive and loving throughout my entire childhood, You are an amazing mom! I dont know what I would do without you. I love you very much!

Dr. Kuhn

Dr. Kuhn thank-you for being so kind and supportive for the past eight years! I am so glad to have you in my life, I love you very much!

Dad

Dad. Thank you for always being there, for being supportive and great at making steaks! HAHAHA! I have enjoyed everyday with you no matter the circumstances. Love you!

Concha, Chelo & Sofie

Thank-you for being amazing sisters! Yall are so supportive and the best sisters in the entire world! I dont know what I would do without yall! I love yall! <3

Aunt Dalia

Tia Dalia. I love you so much. You have always been my favorite aunt! I adore you! I know this year has been hard for you, which hurts me because I love you so much, and it's hard to see someone you care about go through something devastating. I know that you are tough and can stay positive! I love you!

Lou & Enrique

Thankyall for being so supportive and amazing! Even when it's the hardest. I love yall very much!

My Friends!

To my friends that were mentioned in
my book, I am so happy that y'all are
a part of my life! I love y'all!
Thank-you for being amazing friends!

Monica Browning

Tia Monica, thank-you for always
being so sweet and supportive! I love
you very much and wish you lived
closer to me so I could see you more
often!

Ama & Apa

Ama and Apa. Thank-you for being amazing grandparents, being supportive, loving, and kind!<3

Grandma Isabel and Pop

Thankyou Pop and Grandma Isabel for being very supportive and always sweet. I miss yall very much!<3

Follow Bo!

Bo Rodriguez

Social Media

Instagram: @Borodriguez123
Snapchat: @Borodriguez123
Twitter: @Borodriguez123

Lightning Source UK Ltd.
Milton Keynes UK
UKHW022333170119

335721UK00009B/129/P

9 781389 248016